It's All In The Blood

Carol J Forrester

To Liz,

Thank you for all your support,
I hope you enjoy the collection.

 x

ISNB: 9781699630440

This book is dedicated to my grandmother, my grandfather, and my great-grandmother. People who have passed but still walk with me each day.

Content

Poems In The Undercurrent

It's as if someone forgot to turn the radio off.
Not in this room,
but the one across the hall, or down the corridor,
in a somewhere that can't be found
no matter how many corners are checked
or drawers overturned.

The distance turns voices to static,
punctures partial comments,
slipped between floorboards,
strings of mists on summer mornings.

Even if I press my ear to the wallpaper,
I can't link the lines into one another.
The harder I try
the deeper the crackle in the speakers.

I busy myself,
turn the dishwasher on,
boil the kettle,
fill the house with the rattle and clatter
of things needing to be done.

A hiccup in the static leaves a sentence
pressed against my ear
burrowing its way through
to reach the next line
in the mess of grey matter inside.
All the while the radio continues playing
in a room I cannot find.

Grandfather

My grandfather stoops
kisses me briefly.
Hands joined behind his back
while he watches the yard
over my shoulder.

The house and its open door,
my grandmother waiting
on the steps with her smile
and the dog
turning circles
across the tarmac.

Even like this he is tall,
taller than anyone else
in this family
except perhaps his brother
whose mannerisms
are a mirror, if not a match.

Inside,
he retreats to the chair
and the television,
channel 426,
Racing Post in lap,
and tea strong
with just a touch of milk,
the last of the pot.

When I leave
he will look to accept my kiss
as I take my turn to bend,
tell him that I love him
and it will not be long
until I come again.

Young Explorers

My mother's garden tools
rarely found their way home.
She was required to recover them
from the excavation sites
of long-lost cities
my sister and I explored
on summer days
that ended with muddy fingers,
scraped knees,
and soil streaked shins
turning the bathwater brown.

Somehow,
I coerced my sister into digging,
while I counted treasure.
Shards of blue patterned crockery
glaze spiderwebbed by age.
Pieces too small to puzzle together
but surely priceless.

Another Time-Team feature
to be slotted into a drawing
of what had once been beautiful,
that could still be imagined.

We slipped sun softened into sleep
when finally coaxed inside.
I dreamed of the digging places,
things we'd stashed into safe places,
forgotten, lost, and found places.

Second Hand Blades

My mother shaves her legs
with second hand razors.
Breaks them in
on my father's stubble.

Fresh from the packet
they hold too much edge,
too likely to bite
round ankles, over knees,
for her to trust.

In the bath
she strips her shins,
calves,
smooth and hairless.

The men's cost less.
Twenty to a plastic packet
blue and uniformed
like bent necked police
lined up to attention.

She leaves them in the window,
bathroom graveyard
of shampoo bottles
Allen keys
and pennies,
stacked like bonfire kindling.

Cutting Ties

She'd be no nonsense
even at eighteen,
wearing my aunt's features
before they're known as that,
and the same solid expression
as the day I wouldn't eat peas.

If there was a ring
it would be back in its box.
Sealed and hidden
between her palms then his,
unwanted on both sides.

I always imagine them in gateways,
on thresholds and doorways,
untouching, in-between places,
as she says the goodbyes
for both of them.

Her suitcases ready, waiting,
clothes folded into neat squares
and her purses close to hand,
ferry ticket stored safe.

I never thought of her crying,
always dry cheeked, urgent,
keen to get back to the journey
waiting for her on the other side.

I wonder if he asked her to stay,
did he ask more than once?
And was there ever a moment
where the thought of it tempted her.
Or was she already running
from the town by the bog.

Until The Light Gets In

She'd stuff teapots
with carrier bags.
Oranges, blues,
yellow, and pinks,
sunsets in ceramics,
perched on windowsills.

Later,
when they came to pieces
in her hands,
plastic wilted
like dried up petals
she let them fall to dust.

We, the ones left behind
took turns choosing
which to keep.
Shook loose remains
from the curved bone
of these empty bodies.

Found only parts of her.
Enough
that we remembered
some of who she was,
but never quite all.

Earth

At school I learnt how tectonic plates moved,
their shifting, wanderings
always there beneath the earth's skin.
I learnt how the Amazon Rainforest
was considered the lungs of our planet,
and watched presenters with sweat slicked skin
meandering in small wooden boats
along its main, arterial vein.
I learnt that I was part of a predator,
its jaws already closed around the world,
teeth sunk into flesh.
I learnt that I would be needed to do my part
and watched as change
crept along, stuttering and stalling.
I hoped that all the little parts,
would be enough.

A Death In The Family

When his name
stumbles into the conversation
there's a pause,
lag time on memory
a whirling loading screen
as my father explains why
we never saw much of him,
my sister and I.

At work
I warn one of the directors
for when they inevitably speak
to one of my parents.
A death in the family
is generally noted
on client accounts.

Watch him go inwards,
curse and say
'not another one'
both of us unaware
that our ones are one
and we both knew
the same person.

Can't help but think,
there probably is another,
and another,
and another,
and another
just one step from a ledge,
one knot from lifting a rope.

Will their family learn like mine?
A wildfire of gossip

before blood is even told.
One whisper at a bar edge
going up like dry grass
until the countryside is alight
with chatter.

How many more will say,
we knew
this was how things would end.

Sundays

On Sundays
she takes the hollowed bag
from a dozen toilet rolls.
Weighs discarded bottles
one by one.
Slots the empties inside.

Downstairs, Robbie William sings
over the groaning hoover
pushing about
on the sitting room floor,
the scent of burning
as a bobble snags inside.

Once the windowsill is cleared
she empties the wash basket,
uses a towel
to bundle it all
to the kitchen.

Through the window is the dog,
belly stretched across the lawn
in what little there is of sun
this early in a year.

The washing goes into piles,
darks, lights, whites,
work clothes to go on last,
muck stains and dust
delegated to the rear.

Later,
When the mat squelches underfoot,
she'll reach for her tool,
pull the broken beast from its cave

and set to it herself.

Selkie

She slips ashore,
slips her fur
and slips away
to the houses,
the lights,
the people.

I wait,
stumble on shingle
and grasp
for the pelt
abandoned
on the rocks.

The weight of it
still warm
in its thickness
slides heavy
into my lap.

Tease the tangles
across the pads
of my fingertips,
learn the scars
the imperfections.

Shuck the clothes
from my shoulders,
shiver
in the silver
of moonlight.

Tell myself
it will only be
one night.

Farmer's Daughter

Home, I walk the lane with my mum
to see the lambs
leaping from their mothers' backs
onto the straw covered floors,
in the shed penned into wards,
for mothers, new-borns, and expecting.

She stops outside, puts her hands to her hips,
counts the three carcases laid by the door
and curses.

As a child I grew up thinking sugar
was a swear word.

I let her go to them alone,
aware that dead things still scare me,
and they shouldn't really.

But some distances fix like cement
despite the sensible voice in my head
saying there's nothing to hurt you here.

She places her trainer on one's skull,
turns it enough to read the tag
that will confirm what she knows.

In the shed behind the bale wall,
there is bleating.
When mum enters, I follow,
face fixed towards a sound
rather than where the dead sheep lie.
I am not my mother.

How do I think
I can call myself a farmer's daughter.

Newborn

It all takes too long.
Sheep too narrow, lamb too big,
rain hammering on a tin roof
scattering the quiet.

Sunrise still sulks out of sight,
out of mind.
The farmyard a black mirror,
midden cloaked in shadows
until the security light catches
on a fox scurrying for shelter.

Knelt in the straw,
concrete cold on her knees,
her breath is mist.
Knuckles tucked between
the new-born's ankles
as she pulls it free.

She lays it straight,
rubs a fistful of bedding
to its ribcage.
Tries to scrub breath
back into its body.

Twenty miles away,
her own child will be sleeping.
Her husband's mother
holding her place
until Spring runs its course.

She lays the lamb by the door,
notes to call Bradshaw's
in the morning
and tries not to carry it home

to the empty room
where the cot is waiting.

Expectant

"She's expecting Gran to call,
to tell her you're pregnant."

To this
I cannot be anything but accepting
because she's not the only one
expecting
me to announce I'm expecting,
so I must be accepting
that this is the logical progression
in my line of life.

I will split myself,
turn inside out
for another.

That is what I will do.

That is what I want.

This is my dangerous choice.

It will ask me to take my heart,
place it in a basket
and pray rivers don't run red.

As my mother's daughter
the calculation of generations
is on my side
for her the slipknot had tightened
on the idea of another pregnancy.

But I could be an echo
of my grandmothers.
Could lose it early,

carry an uncertainty
for fifty years.

Could lose it later
but too far from help
so the alarm
is not a warning
but a death knell.

If I scream out a girl
will she carry this blood
into her own womb?
Find new rapids
to break herself upon?
Will she even scream at all?

Alarm

Ropes of smoke curling
along the banister
towards the bedrooms.

There is no detector,
starved hollow,
its open mouth yawning.

A window
sticking on the paintwork
yelps when opened.

Winter spits in,
wake up call of ice
and air cruel to be kind.

Yanks us from sleep,
to the oil burn clinging
at the back of our throats.

Narrow escape
all for a phone call
splitting the silence.

Old Fears

You catch me by the armpits
and lift me body, whole
into the air.

It's the same as earlier
when you closed a hand
around my wrist,
grip locked on.

But you were turned away
to the lad in a new judo gi
and I muted the scream
snapped the lid back on a memory
turned my tremble to laughter.

You were not them,
this was not danger,
only a joke
unaware of the shadows
behind my smile
designed not to frighten
you…

designed not to let you know
that I was afraid.

In The Kitchen

It was a game
to try and sneak past
the motion detector
hunkered in the top corner
of every room.

Barefoot,
despite the scolding
we would catch if caught,
we slid sole stuck
across the kitchen tiles.

Red eyed
it saw us flinch,
flashed in triumph,
told us we were not invisible.

Instead of infrared
we imagined lasers,
crisscrossed
along the corridor.

I held a handstand
for three seconds,
then toppled
so tried again
until my face bloomed
blush.

Gave up on sneakery,
sprinted the length
of the house
in one breath
catapulted back.

Got told off,
told to slow down.
Apologised,
tried again,
toppled,
did not slow down.

Against All The Signs

I stopped believing in harbingers,
in the same way I try not to flinch
when passing on the stairs,
or attempt to hide a sidestep
for cracks in the pavement.

Superstition crawled inside my head
before I was old enough to name it.
Caught up between pie crusts
and the turning coils
of apple peels.

"Good Day Mr Magpie,
are you well? How's the family?"

Years ago
we buried glass
when it broke like ice.
My mother feared
lessons she'd been fed
might just come true.

Seven years bad luck
unless it's hidden.
Deeper now, deeper,
lose the evidence,
forget the thought.

Crossed knives,
tempest in a teapot,
do not stir and do not pour
these quarrelsome ideas,
protect the family you love.

They will always come in threes.
The worst of it unseen.

Intimacy Illogical

Intimacy is illogical
she thinks,
while counting credit lines
on a sitting room T.V,
the new *boyfriend*
sandwiched between her
and the cushions.

He can't be comfortable,
with her cutting off circulation
to the arm still coiled
across her shoulders.

And there are shoulder blades
cutting in,
where she's lying,
ribs like slats on a single bed.

This is like, not love, not even lust,
with a guy
already bounding ahead
in a false-start relationship
she's not sure she wants.

When she calls me
I want to say, "that is not intimacy",
that it is mimicry.
It's fake it till you make it
and hope if it quacks like a duck,
if it looks like a duck,
then it is love.

And no,
you may never want his hand
or his arm,

or the space along his hip.
They may not be your places,
but you will find places
and they will fit.

Countryside Wisdom

Always greet red dawns with caution.

Farmer's daughter,
I turn countryside sayings over
and over
like hard-boiled sweets
in my mouth.

Syrup long since sucked
from the centre,
they are crunch and brittle.
shards prick my gums
in warning.

No amount of scoffing,
will keep my grandmother
from speaking to the dawn.

Soft, familiar,
she chants the same song,
myth now made fact.

Red mornings,
beautiful
and looming.

We should watch
for a change in the winds.

Wrung Out

Today is a tumble dryer day,
where I fall from the drum
crumpled, creased, confused,
humming with static,
limbs limp with heat,
and one sharp shock
from folding altogether.

This Was Supposed To Be A Love Poem

We are all born of someone else
that doesn't make us servants.

This stretch of red called fate,
I stretched it to the snapping point,
wrenched it
and myself.
Mopped up the evidence with your shirt.

The vicar explains the service.
Says traditionally no one uses
'honour and obey'
these days.

So I do not honour you.
I am not made of you
or made for you
but this, this is, this is...
the words for it escape me
and I am normally
so good with words.

But true, true enough
I will not obey, as you will not obey.

I plant a foot against your spine
dig my fingers between your ribs.
Is one missing?
Would it explain this inability
to imagine or remember
how I was me before you.

I think I am still myself.

I hope I am still myself.

When you come back to bed
I am sorry
and I am angry
and I am all the things
I cannot express to anyone
else.

I count your ribs again.
then count my own.

Red Dress

In the calm of an empty room
I found Pride behind the mirror's glass
and coaxed it into daylight.

Flames fanned from ash
with a slip of red silk
slashed open, white to the skin,
bare like orange pith.

But Pride slipped from my shoulders
just beyond an open doorway,
gnawed a hollow in my belly,
burrowed down deep, and dark,
and out of reach.

Then in the mirror
were only shadows and shame
grey once more
with the reassurance
that no one and everyone
would have been looking anyway.

Questions I Still Have

Was I a plaster
you slapped on
to cover the burns
left by your family?
Something temporary,
to hide the harm.

Was he water?
More than you'd seen
all in one place
and so inviting
you were willing
to drown.

Did you lose me
on purpose?
Or did the currents
just pull us apart?

Either way,
did you notice
that I was gone?

Trousers

I do not wear the trousers,
instead I choose pairs
from the ones that still fit
since the last time I braved
changing rooms
in shops with bright lights
and badly drawn curtains.

He does much the same,
but focuses on which ones
have enough pockets
to reduce back and forths
from ladder to toolbox
without dragging waistbands
from his hips.

I am warding off razor blades
and the efforts of shaving
or the efforts of showing
that I grow hair too.

I am the battler of cropped legs,
tactical shin shaves,
belly pats, sucked in stomachs,
and old favourites
that hold in all the bits
which jiggle in judgment.

Pockets come sewn shut,
too small for much more
than a hand, or a tissue,
unless you run the risk
of ruining the cut.

More so than less,

the trousers wear me.

I am not wearing the trousers.

These trousers wear me.

Home Bird

These wings don't go far,
or high much.
They rustle the leaves
in the hedge
when summer sits about,
or crackle the branches
when summer has flit south.

There is something to be said
for roots over wings.
For a spot to return to
each time,
when it's warm or cold
and I don't want
to go far or high very much.

Preacher

I listened to a man
speaking of virgins.
How the obedience of one
counter-balanced the disobedience
of the other.
Names became irrelevant,
as he stripped them down
to the space
between their thighs.

Legs Eleven

The other day I changed twice before work,
pillaged the wardrobe like a robber
searching for redemption among my flaws,
till the hangers lay as broken bones
between the rucks and folds of bedding
behind me.

It takes one conversation
to reduce a woman to the worth of her shape.
Words passed on like school notes,
in hushed tones
with the advice to be more careful
and perhaps wear tights to hide skin,
if I was going to wear that dress again.

It became a replay of every word spoken
to me, around me, about me, that day.
Had I missed the tone in the kitchen
when a colleague asked
if I was not cold
and I shrugged past smiling
mug in hand, more focused on me
and how the dress put power
in my step.

Treating limbs like traitors,
the wardrobe offers reprimands
instead of comfort.
Too tight, too short, too sheer,
and this no longer sits as it should
though I'm sure it did yesterday.

Late,
everything goes back in haphazard,
settling on something

that shouldn't raise complaint
or contempt
but still sits strange on my frame
as I test the stretch in the fabric
to see how much more, I can hide.

It is all a lesson in marketing.
I simply do not know
how to package myself right.

Made A Vase

I am made a vase.
Told how prettily
I clutch these petals
between my lips,
draw the stems deep
into me.

I am background
to the room.
Placed out the way,
on mantel, dresser,
windowsill.
A lovely afterthought.

Empty,
I become clutter
put aside
to a dark place.
In exile
till flowers bloom again.

Megera

They name me
jealous one.
Plait snakes through my hair,
till it rises about my shoulders
a mane of venom.

Perhaps this is true enough.

They say I crush men,
the ones who come to me
through their own will
and actions.
Lay the cruelty of betrayal
at my feet.

I am not my sisters,
blood avenger, unceasing
in pursuit.
I am an emotion painted
upon every action
I set forth.

I am furious and bright,
burning beyond recognition
till they shield their eyes
and call me ugly.

I am a woman of power.

Since The Beginning

Despite Eve,
we don't seem to know evil.
Unless the fruit of knowledge lied
or we've become very good
at making others' sins our own
with a: 'Yes but…'
and 'you've got to take it
as it was meant.'
Perhaps that too was Eve's curse,
after the pains of childbirth
they gave her the weight
of Adam's sins as well,
like pebbles building inside her
until the stones sink her
and still they can say she's to blame
because she was led astray first.
After all,
she realised her nakedness before him,
she was asking for it since the beginning.

Sanctity

Armoured, escorted
she takes entry of a sacred space,
told the bleed between her legs
is a stain that won't come out.

Another speaks of crimes
only to find punishment
on a rooftop
when she dares to hold.

To become a woman
means to be an exile,
a cycle turned a curse,
proof that this sex is unworthy.

Honour becomes a blade
against noisy girls,
who forget
their place.

Voices rise when ink spills.
A drop for the ocean,
to make her a story.
a rally cry.

But it does not bring her back,
the doors do not open,
dams does not break,
only groan a little.

Changes is always too late
for the child burning on a roof,
the daughter begging for justice.
A girl asking to be a person.

Changing Room

I do not fit.

The flesh in my chest
bulges under my arms
until I have wings,
like a dodo.

The hanger,
spat on the floor
protests that it should
indeed be right
for me.

I am the one wrong,
the one shaped incorrect.
Proportions thrown out
by a lottery
of heritage.

My breasts refuse
to sit pretty,
and the strap
at my back
plays at a garotte.

I think my ribs will crack.

But maybe that's the way?

New Year Run

When I admitted that I'd shaved my armpits
especially
M- fist pumps the air,
Shows off her fuzzy winter warmers
before sidestepping a walker
trailing yet another small dog
more interested in us than its walk.

This January,
was warmer than expected.

I cursed Christmas for clinging
to the places idleness had already marked
as problem areas.

M- woops, revels in her freedom,
finds a stride I struggled to match.

She smiles with her whole face,
lights up
and bounces
one foot to the other,
sprung for the last stretch home,
waiting for me to conquer this hill
between us.

Earlier
this had seemed like such a good idea.

An Ever-Changing Beast

'We should really address the elephant in the room.'
Those were the words you tossed out over coffee,
like spare change or old candy wrappers,
between the books and the plant pots.
There didn't seem to be much point explaining,
your elephant wasn't in this room,
or hadn't been until you kicked up dust clouds
into a grey silhouette.
I kept my silence on the matter,
much like you had kept yours until now,
too cautious about stirring sleeping beasts.
About how you might have to hold me together
when all the pieces broke apart
and ran for the corners in the skirting,
rats abandoning ship
at the first sign of storms.
I let you think you were the only one
holding out a hand,
while you explained why I was sad
and how it could all be fixed
if I tried hard enough
and put in the work.
I've learned to listen to the some speeches
without really hearing them.
It's the same trick you used each time I tried
to put shadows into sentences.

Sunsets

When you asked me if I liked it,
I pretended to smile
and told you it was beautiful.
I did not mention it was different
to the ones back at home,
where gritty haze doesn't hang
morning, eve, and night,
and the hum of silence
echoes differently in the darkness
and I think for a moment
you believed the words,
despite the wet on my cheeks
and your hand loose in mine.

Jörmungandr

I'll start at the toes,
short,
and not quite in joint
with one another.

Pause around the ankles.
Suckle them
like gobstoppers
to the marrow.

Crunch shin and calf,
ravish thighs
till the fat glistens
along my jawbone.

Pick the pelvis clean,
pop each ovary
between thumb
and forefinger.

Still juicy and ripe.

Pull intestines,
lungs, liver, heart,
kidneys free.
Mince into a pie.

Portion each breast
out with the cuts
to ensure a moist
cook.

Lick the remains clean
from each finger.
Grind the bones

between my teeth.

Leave one hand for eyeballs,
seasoned tongue
tastes a lot like ox,
ears more like bacon.

At the end,
begin again.

Safe Harbour

I have always made for safe harbour,
the sort where you dock ships
with rotten decks and broken masts
close to sinking.

These moorings are good. Constant.
I'm used to others setting up camp
on the slopes of these beaches,
leaving litter on the sands.

Clearing the clutter takes strength,
after the ones who came and went
like hurricanes howling their pain,
all to then sail on calmer.

I let you carve out a bolt hole,
but now it is not needed.
I realise you never came ashore
for anything but rescue.

I wonder if your maps still mark me
as a place with a name like home.

Where The Water Breaks

There's a sheen to the water,
a swirl of slick, slurp, sludge
squirming up the beach
surfing old tidal rips
to suck down feathered flurries,
their bone stuck wings
submerged to make stones
with panicked beady eyes,
staring up at a surface
mirroring
startled starlings swooping
in a grey choked sky
and a small child
with a face still plump young,
trying to break the glass
with one fat finger,
all the while calling
for his mother to come
and look.

Echoes

Unfurled
you settled yourself in this house.
I kept finding pieces of you
in places I was sure you'd never touched,
under the edge of a lampshade,
in a socket behind the television,
between boxes inside the attic,
along the grain of the floorboards.
Safe places became the most dangerous,
and when your smile
found its way between the spines of two books
I turned every shelf I owned to kindling.
Move the offending volumes
to opposite ends of the house
and tore out the pages that looked most like you.
It didn't help.
You still echoed in the chimney
when the wind howled just right.

Like You

These weren't your clothes
though they looked alike.
You were not inside them,
pressed up against the seams
in that half-contained way
you always wore yourself,
spilling out beyond your limits.

The store assistant didn't fold
in the way you would have,
but store assistants don't,
they fold in that flip, flip manner
quarters, then eights,
small enough to post
inside a square plastic bag.

At home they looked different,
changed on a second glance
and not as they had appeared
in the shop floor lights
under mannequins perched
as frightened birds
about to topple.

Like wire, I bent myself
into shapes that mimicked you.
Stretched fabric
across angles and bones,
till I was taut as a drum
or tambourine.
Beat a rhythm you would have,
and tried marching
to a different tune.

Ugly Duckling

Some days I want to step out of myself,
pass the reigns over and leave
every text message you have sent me
exactly as it is,
unread,
unwanted,
unneeded.
You do not tell a swan how to swim,
you trust it enough
to keep paddling
even when the water holds like a mirror
clear enough to reflect your worries
to anyone watching.
I know I am not a swan,
I'm something closer to a goose
honking at the picnic tables
and chasing after children.
I still swim just as well though
so do not tell me
I need to worry about being left behind,
I'm getting there in my own damn time.

Crewe In April

The sunshine shifts dull brown to caramel
over the tulips and the daffodils
their heads tipped aside
in slow lazy waves
to a cloud scuppered sky
with its deceptive sheen of blue.

Sale boards sprout like snowdrops
at the ends of gardens.
A row of them, an ellipse,
or a full stop.

The billboard by the station changes
and the ticket machine flashes
out of order,
but not the flag outside the Box,
writhing in the wind
perhaps a quarter of what it once was.

With wire wool hair like Einstein,
the man in the red Defender smokes,
watches the pedestrian lights turn.
The vehicles draw to a stop,
he takes his chance and moves
a fraction of an inch.

In the bay windows of next door
there is a gap in the curtains
and a new vase
with purple flowers.
Plastic but pretty.

In Contradiction

I have been treated like glass before
coddled in a way that set my teeth on edge,
pushed me close enough to biting
that my mouth flooded with salvia.

Funny.

Metal is beaten into shape,
heated until it loses itself to the fire
and then quenched into permeance.

Did you think I was still melting?
Still too malleable?

Was it after the accident?
or before?
My uncle ordered me not to cry
because now was not the time.

But it was the time.
It really fucking was,
and swallowing the knot in my throat
left my insides tangled
still.

Instead I learned to laugh.
Laughter comes easily in stress now.
Pops like fairy liquid bubbles
from my gullet.

Do you like the colours?
This sheen of oil swollen between us,
close enough to reach,
to burst.

All the while,
I am so damn close to breaking
and so very, very unbreakable
it hurts.

Do you understand what I mean?

If you treat me like glass again
I will bite,
but please,
when I ask,
help me pick up the pieces.

Back Through The Blood

We come from sheep thieves
and cattle rustlers,
according to my grandfather.

My mother teases, tells my dad
'at least my ancestors went to war
dressed in more than paint.'

Supposedly there's a thread
pulling us to the doomsday book,
a landing where her maiden name
came ashore.

Even earlier, we were Viking,
raiders and warriors,
shield maidens and soothsayers.

How many gods has this blood
worshipped?
How many prayers
addressed to someone different?

I grew up in draught riddled churches,
all stone and pine, choirs singing
from the space beside the organ.
Greenmen now curios, oddities,
tucked away among the rafters.

Will that be the faith I pass on?

We have learnt what is proper,
this generation, and the one before.
How far back do I need to trace
to find berserkers screaming
in their war colours,

streaking towards the bogland?

Am I allowed to call them kin?

Words

I.

For a while I carried words like weapons.
Saw them only for their sharpened edges
the ways in which they sliced,
left mouths open, and gasping,
burrowed into the skin.
I had enough scars of my own,
to show how dangerous words could be.
Learnt where to aim for,
which veins bleed the most.

II.

Anger can only burn on a short fuse.
It consumes too quickly,
fizzles out before it fueled you.
Leaves you wondering why
the knives are slick with your blood.
No one warns about the energy
that pain steals,
how hollowness swallows whole
everything you built of yourself.

III.

Healing is so much slower.
On nights when I'm awake and he is not
I pick words out of my skin,
the ones I pretend I forgot.
I turn them over in the blue light
Of the router on the nightstand,
try to decode the handwriting,
too distant to be distinct.
I will tell myself I am older,

wiser,
more mature.
I will pretend I do not hurt any more.

First Dance

The DJ tried passing on pointers
and moved your hand along my waist
before concluding you a lost cause
and beating a hasty retreat
to the background of his booth.

You,
smirking on whisky and laughter
launched into the music
with the same caution as a rally driver
coming into the last bend
in first place.

Witness to all of this
the sparkle of camera phone flashes
our guests watched us spin,
and I watched you forget them
like confetti once it's fallen
and the cheers have gone quiet.

In the swirls of my dress,
your arms kept me upright.
Both unsteady
we kept each other's feet beneath,
each other's heads above.

Is that not what it means
to be in love.

Tongue And Cheek

The slow, relaxed kisses,
often led to something else
less slow, less relaxed,
less clothed
more time consuming,
all consuming.
While the sharp, sweet pecks
always on the way past
like commas in conversation,
were the pauses for breath
anchoring us to each other.

Girls Night

Despite the clumsy introduction
I was flattered when he offered
to replace the drink he'd spilled
by crashing into me.

Despite the flush of attention,
the idea that engagement
made me desirable,
I said no.

Despite the smile, the wine,
the press of cheek to cheek,
us fighting to be heard
over speakers pumping

I caught his comment.

Offered me *all night drinks*
if I just hook him up
with the blonde
to my right.

"Not that you're not hot,"
but blondes were his thing,
until the blonde said 'no',
until the round brought him back
to the girl with the ring.

Until I pointed it out,
the band on my finger
the man back at home,
then it was three strikes out
and the boy was gone.

Does it make me shallow

to be annoyed
I wasn't first choice?
Does it make me shallow
to be annoyed
I wasn't first choice?

The Way Things Go

It came down suddenly one night,
stumbled on a storm
and slipped its supports.

Stubborn in its place
it managed a little shelter,
kept out some rain,
not a lot.

We left it lopsided,
a loose tooth
we were unprepared to test
fear it come free entirely.

Behind wild grass gone to seed
and wooden pallets
stacked crooked inside one another
from rot
it looked in-keeping.

Turning the way of time
and history.

On Our Last Day In Japan

To hurry us home,
the sky split its seams.
Tried to wash us
into the subway line.
Tried to turn rail to river,
Tokyo to Venice.
Tried to sweep us
altogether from the city,
to cleanse any trace of us
from it.

Zeus Is Spear Fishing Over Stranraer

Poseidon will make a game of it,
swell the seas up the shoreline,
drive the fish deeper
than Zeus can catch.

He does not care for the why
of his brother being here tonight,
what he's done to anger Hera now,
who he must have taken to bed.

This boils back to the before times,
when his world was small
and dark
and close.

Before Zeus gave him the oceans,
held the gift of it in his hands
like a toad or a coloured stone,
some trivial discovery.

Poseidon did not grasp the vastness,
the difference to his father's belly.
How cold the waters close
around solitary limbs.

It had been a war,
it had been a sea of bloodshed,
but still there had been three
to steer a path to land.

He lets Zeus win a strike,
splits waves on a knife edge
of coastline,
foam fireworks flickering upwards.

Storms always blow themselves out,
lightning does not last forever.
When the seas settle in the morning
there will be no gods to be found.

If I Were…

If I were Mrs Dalloway,
I'd buy the flowers myself,
or perhaps I'd steal them
like Offred.
Only one,
a dying one.
Closest to the end of bloom
but still displayed in the sitting room,
and maybe, just maybe
I could become flora too,
and shed flesh for blossom
for broom and meadowsweet
or even daisies
which could be plucked
petal by petal
to the thin green core
and tossed aside
when it was not beautiful
anymore.

In The Garden

The peas have podded. I'm not sure if it's the snap, or your
bog standard, good old trusty garden type, but they've podded
first with the white petals of the flowers still stuck to the green
of their shells.

Inside the crop is still too small, too young. I checked today.
Popped my nail into the seam, slit through the flesh, cracked it
open. New growth, old book. They both sound the same.

They are not ready for harvest, but when you bite down they
explode. They taste like spring, or summer, or something else
that's hot days and sudden rain storms. They tasted like they
should do.
New and fresh.

It's been a wet one,
this spring, this downpour of water
thickening the green.

Persephone

There are gulls circling,
looking almost clean
against unbroken blue
of a rare summer day
in England.

It's not tropics hot
though the wind's lost her edge
gone soft
now Spring's worked in
and smoothed over
last season's fall out.

It's not all plain sailing.
Summer, Spring,
both blow hot, cold,
in a place like this.
Never quite sure
what it is they want.

Still, it's not snow in June.
This scatter or row boats
beached up on the shingle
are no autumn fall.
Today is a summer in full,
another day of waiting
for the season to set.

Don't Call It Healing

Coping does not need to be pretty,
instead it will raise an ugly head,
lift out of the shadows
when you are at peace to wallow
in the echoes of a memory
and remind you
you are a person
with things to do,
places to be
and lingering too long
is not an option.
Instead it will drag you
back over
the broken pieces of yourself
all the while refusing
to let you bend
at the spine,
or buckle
at the knees.
It moves you forward
inch by bruising inch
no matter the scars it leaves.

Glacial

For a millennium you were glacial.
Slid oh so slow
through dirt, and stone,
turned mountains into valley paths,
cracked plains, made them seas.

We watched the snow fall,
smother you until we forgot,
blinked stunned
when the sun shucked your coat
and the light made you shine.

Change creeps closer in millimetres,
presses the before away carefully,
slips itself into spaces
that hastiness would break.

Bard On Blore Heath

One paragraph for all the lost bodies,
somewhere still beneath dirt and grass
and the slow trundle of grazing cattle
meandering, one fence line to another.

Musket balls plucked up with conkers,
rolled across a palm like a marble,
dropped into a Tupperware tub,
they outlasted the bones and flesh.

A field with five hundred years to forget
yet the calf gets sick with lead
loses its eyesight to a pellet
from a gun fired half a millennium before.

History reaches past its paragraph
of three thousand nameless men.
Another misery of litter
leftover once the war was done.

Persephone (No. 2 - Homecoming)

You must come home,
you must, you must, you must,
because I say so,
because I am the grown-up
and you are the child.

So come home,
to the house that still smells
like safety, and nostalgia,
and stagnation.

Come see your mother
whose bones have turned
to winter branches
in cruel irony of a ransom
she held the world to.

Half-wonder if her skin
won't simply come away,
leave a suit of her
for you to step inside.
Fulfil her last and first wish.

Breath in that scent
of sweet peas and summer roses
pressed between the bed sheets.
Pretend that she still holds it
on her skin.

Pretend that she was other
than your mother
who would not let go
no matter how you struggled,
or how far you ran.

Let her think that this is forever.
Know that she will pass
before the leaves turn
and your duty to her will end
at last.

A Life Like Helios

I followed your path,
at a distance.

You like the sun,
or any volatile star
burning a streak
towards the horizon.

A scorching vision
to those of us
watching, waiting,
aware that you would set
before us.

Terrified of dusk.

Sensing its arrival
anyway.

Bloom

When you arrived as the snowdrops melted,
pressed cherry blossom to my breast,
told me love is like a flower in bloom,
already closer to an end than the start.

Pressed cherry blossom to my breast,
found thorns that left their marks,
already closer to an end than the start
when sorrow grew from these seeds.

Found thorns that left their marks,
taught me how to cut out dead wood,
when sorrow grew from these seeds
pruning became vital to overall survival.

Taught me how to cut out dead wood,
told me love is like a flower in bloom,
pruning became vital to overall survival
when you arrived as the snowdrops melted.

Standing The Test

Cup the whole of me in one hand.
Hold my belly up to a light,
judge my origins,
if I might be the real deal.

Examine my spine carefully
through this sheen of skin
while I burn like paper,
edges curling in as I smoke.

Test me between teeth,
bite down, heads up,
crack your enamel
on my silver forked tail.

Spit me free
with blood and tooth
and every question asked
to test the mettle in me.

Wonder why I leave
with a word like love
so sour in my mouth
I choke.

Balance For Better

Keep your balance and your wits
grasped tight.
Knot them between your fingers
like purse straps
when the street empties to darkness
and even the lamplight
does little to chase away shadows.
There's no rescuing dignity
if you spill,
heels caught in the rickets
of this ladder we've built
from the bones of those who wept
behind closed doors.
Emotion would prove them woman
and that was weakness,
still is
in the eyes of some.
So the *weak* gift their spines and prayers,
hollow themselves into armour
for the next generation,
and the one after that,
in a desperation that they will be the drop
that tips the scales to even.

Trickle Down

Even in a landlocked county,
it all flows back to water.
Wells bursting into lakes,
to spurn greedy landlords,
women sunk beneath them
with pondweed for hair.

Even in a landlocked county,
it all flows back to women
sunk deep into a Lady's path
beyond the reach of light.
They come for the children,
for the men who bathe at night.

They toll the bells in warning,
they toll the bells in spite,
because what else do women have
but bile and bitter bright.

Acknowledgments

When I graduated from university and got my first full-time job, my mother warned me that it would be easy for me to put the writing aside and get swept up in the new. She told me to make sure I didn't loose that side of me.

I have been lucky enough to grow up in a family of people who cheer your successes and pick you up when you don't quite hit the mark. I must thank all of them for their endless support, and for putting up with every poem that I subjected them to.

This book would not exist without the help of family and wonderful friends. My mother who ensured I wouldn't lose my words to work, my sister who stepped in when I was ready to give up, Helen Kay who gave her time to read and feedback on each poem, and Caroline who designed a superb cover for this book.

I would also like to thank the wonderful creative communities in Shrewsbury and Crewe who have given me the confidence to put my writing out into the world and have been kind enough to share their own wonderful work with me.

I am so grateful to you all.

Carol J Forrester lives in Cheshire with her husband, and spends her free time writing, reading, and practicing judo.

You can find out more about her and her work at
www.caroljforrester.com

Printed in Poland
by Amazon Fulfillment
Poland Sp. z o.o., Wrocław

62417754R00059